THE HISTORY OF THE UNIVERSE

Revised Edition

Scientist believe in the big bang theory. Yes it is true but they do not know exactly how the big bang took place. Let me explain to you how the big bang theory took place. There was space and there was outer space and underneath space there was inner space. Now outer space was more dense than space and was forcing itself through the pores in space from the outside. As a result of outer space putting weight on space the weight of the two together made inner space more dense than space and was forcing itself through the pores in space from the inside of space. When the chemicals from outer space met the chemicals from inner space there was chemical element change. Since space was not a conductor of the chemical element changes. These chemical element changes had to have a release for their by products which is radiation Since these by products are more dense than space they are causing space to expand.

Saturn compared to our earth is 100,000 times bigger than our earth. Then our sun is 100,000 times bigger than Saturn. Again there are stars 100,000 times bigger than our sun. Our sun is a star that supplies the earth with light during the day. Stars have different sizes as well as different colors. These different colors show us what stage of life the star is in. Stars have the following colors white, blue, yellow and red. If a star is white it is a hot star and the beginning of it's life. If the star is blue it is on the second stage of it's life. If a star is yellow it is on the third stage of it's life. If a star is red it is on the fourth stage of it's life. At end of the red stage of the stars life the star explodes and leaves a black hole.

Over the years till to today's date. Scientists nowadays measure time in light years and that is based on how fast and how far light travels in one year. In The U.S.A. and Canada one year is based on one circumference that the earth travels around the sun.

Now scientists know that the earth has a life span of 600,000,000,000 years. They also know that half of it has passed and has another 300,000,000,000 years to go.

Scientist also know how life started on the earth. Since lighting is seven times hotter than the surface of our sun when lighting struck water it altered the chemical elements of the water and made a life form that was able to take in chemicals to maintain itself and pass waste out and away, which is chemical element change. Around 300,000,000 years ago dinosaurs were at top of the life on the earth. Things remained this way until 100,000,000 years ago. So you can see that dinosaurs were at the top of the food change for 200,000,000 years. About 100,000,000 years ago there was a huge asteroid that hit the earth and changed the enviroment.

The measurement of time that The U.S.A. and Canada use is based on the calendar that the Romans used. It was used for the time of Jesus Christ and those people that believed in him. Ten percent of the Jewish people believed in him at the same time as some Romans. These people moved upwards to start building countries that are now Europe. Some of The Romans that believed in Jesus Christ were fed to the lions and had no choice but to move in to Europe to avoid being fed to the lions.

It was some time between 300,000,000 years ago when the dinosaurs were at the top of the food chain that the huge asteroid hit the earth about 100,000,000 years ago and took 1/4 of the earth to form our moon. What was on that huge astroid could have been many different types of mammals as well as some humans that were being taught about Jesus Christ and did not know that they were really on a huge space ship that lost its way in space and ended up crashing in to the earth. This caused the enviroment on the earth to change very seriously as only the life forms that were able to change with the changing enviroment on the earth were able to survive. It was not the strongest and the smartest that survived but rather those that found it easies to adapt to the enviromental changes on the earth. The smallest part of the universe can only be imagineable. It could be a seed of a tree or a cell waiting to be germinated by a cell of a sperm quite possibly by a human or an insect or what ever type of life form that is being born for the purpose of carrying on the species and at the same time adapting to the changes in the enviroment no matter how small or how big the changes are. How large the universe is can only be imagable as well.

Now we can imagine how small the earth is but what is the earth's position in size and place in the universe. First of all our earth is a planet in our solar system along with nine other planets. One of those planets is Saturn which is 100,000 times bigger than our earth. Then we have our sun which really is a star and it is a dwarf star and it is 100,000 times bigger than Saturn. Then we have stars that are 100,000 times bigger than our sun. The galaxy that we live in is the Milky Way and in the Milky Way we have the Big Dipper and the Little Dipper.

Now in the Milky Way there are billions of solar systems or more. In the universe there are billions of galaxies or more that also have billions of solar systems.

Where we left off was at the huge asteroid hitting the earth 100,000,000 years ago and changing the enviornment drastically. Some dinosaurs became birds others became alligators and crocodiles others snakes, turtles etc. Now some mammals became seals, whales, dolphins others became groundhogs, mice, rats, squirrels. The people that were on the huge asteroid and were being taught about Jesus Christ and did not know about other mammals. After the huge asteroid crashed into the earth the people that were taught about Jesus Christ had seen for the first time other mammals. As the officers in charge of the huge asteroid knew how to exist on the earth they had the knowledge for the people to survive. The officers had previous experience and knew how to hunt and survive on the earth. The officers taught the young men how to hunt while the young ladies were taught how to cook and take care of babies. As the small commnuity was running out of food the young men and the young ladies got married and left the commnuity in order to find more food. After that, every so often the commnuities got together for song and dance and other young couples got together to build other commnuities. After a while there were disagreements over sex, religion and politics. This system carried on until 4,000 B.C. and the Life of Jesus Christ which was 35 years and another 35 years before the New Testament was written which is now 2011 years A.D. for a total of 6011 years. Which is greater 6011 years or 100,000,000 years and I do think that you will choose the second.

Now we are at 4,000 B.C. which is 4,000 years before Jesus Christ. At that time the Jewish people were slaves building the pyramids for the Egyptians. One day there was a Jewish lady who had a baby and put him in a basket so he could be found and live a life with out being a slave. He was found by some Egyptians and was raised to be a Pharaoh. His name was Moses and when he learned that his people the Jewish people were working as slaves to build the pyramids he did not like this fact. So what he did was to keep the logs hollowed out and holes to make the stones that were going to the top of the pyramids lighter and easier to get there. Near the bottom of the pyramids the logs were hollowed out but without holes in the bottom of the logs as they had more weight to support. Now Moses' idea was to leave the hollowed logs without the holes in the bottom of the logs down by the Red Sea and one night Moses lead the Jewish people in the hollowed out logs with out the holes in the logs to start crossing the Red Sea. Naturally the Egyptians started following the Jewish people but little did the Egyptians not realize that the logs that they were in had been hollowed out and had holes in the bottom as well and they sank in to the Red Sea.

After Moses led the Jewish people away from Egypt he went on top of a mountain on a cloudy day and lit a fire and brought down the Ten Commandmands and he told the Jewish people that God told him what to write. To his suprise when he came back down from the mountain the Jewish people offered him a golden calf and Moses told the Jewish people to melt it down as it was putting gold before the God that Moses knew which was a sin.

Here we are at the beginning of the life of Jesus Christ which is 2046 years ago. We see how Mary met Joesph and how he took her to be his wife even when she was pregant and how Jesus

Christ was born 2046 years ago on the 25 of December. From this we see how he lived and taught what was going to be in the New Testament Bible before it was ever written around 35 years after he died. His life was 35 years for a total of 70 years altogether. The New Testament is 1941 years old and we are in the year 2011 A.D. which stands for after Jesus Christ death.

Jesus Christ taught that if you believed in him being the son of God that if you sinned you could ask him for forgiveness that he would ask his father who is above him to forgive you and let you in to heaven. Jesus also taught that everyone sinned and those who did not believe Jesus not being the son of God that they would not be forgiven but rather go to hell and burn in hell away from God eternally

Here we are now in the year 2011 and every one is looking for Jesus Christ to come back and raise people from the dead and bring heaven along with him. Well take a quick look around on the earth we have dogs, cats we have mice, birds, snakes, insects and spiders we also have trees, fish, whales etc. and the list goes on and on. All of the life forms on the earth are forms of chemical element changes some slower and others faster. All of these life forms will one day have to change in to other chemical elements which humans call death. Now as we see Jesus Christ threaten the people that did not believe in him and did not have any respect for his fellow man they were going to burn in hell with Satan for an eternity seperated from God. The reason that Jesus Christ did this was because people in those days did not have knowledge of electricty and fossil fuels to use this power to better mankind. So if you look around all of those life forms that I mentioned, they all have feelings and have power to make choices the same as mankind either to be good or bad. So all you have to do is treat all animated life forms with respect and hope you receive the same from other men which is heaven on earth while other men take advantage of other men which is hell on earth. And in the long run it shall follow them. I will now prove that Jesus Christ is still alive.

We also know that there were four Jesus Christs but the true one is suppose to be Jesus Christ of Nazerath

We know that Jesus claimed to be the son of God and he was giving his life to forgive us of our sins. He was put to death on the cross and when he was dead the people put him in his cave and put a huge stone in front of the cave. Now scientists know that caves are formed by older rivers that have an entrance and an exit in a mountain. If Jesus Christ's cave was an exit, it would have been possible at the entrance for some older Egyptian with white hair and bronzed feet to come out of the cave on the third day to try and show that Jesus Christ burned in hell with Satan and took away the keys of hell from Satan and rising from the dead to prove that he was truly the son of God and God was more powerful than Satan.

In this section of the book we would like to prove that Jesus Christ is still alive. It takes around 20 years to raise a generation and in 100 years there are 5 generations. Now in the year of 2011 A.D. it takes 100 years divided in to 2011 A.D. to give us 20 1/10 one hundred years and we times 20 1/10 by 5 generations gives us 100 generations of Jesus Christ has been handed down through the years from generation to generation in mind and body.

There are also Mohammed, Buddah, Krishna, Karma and other religions that were passed down from generation to generation that have been conceived on this planet called the Earth.

Now that we realize Jesus Christ is alive and passed on down from generation to generation in mind and body we also now realize that we are in Heaven.

Now supose that I told you that there is a book out called "In The Absence of The Myth". The myth is that there is a God. "In The Absence of The Myth" there is no God.

Can you imagine all of the good things that you could do with your life without worrying about sin and how it does not apply to you any more.

But it does not say that all of Jesus Christ's teachings are a waste of time becauce some of his teachings could be useful even if you do not believe in God such as to treat your fellow man like you want be treated yourself.

That goes for any other religions like Mohammed, Buddha, Krishna, Karma or any other religion that is on the earth.

So now we are in the year 2011 A.D. and as stated above Jesus Christ is still alive. What doctors and scienists know nowaday is that the number one and the number two systems are working together to keep our bodies alive. We will start with the digestive track number two. When we get hungry we look at food and decide what we would like to eat, we decide how we want the food cooked and as we prepare the food our saliva glands start to process chemicals in our mouths to start the break down of the food that we are eating. We chew the food in to smallers pieces of food to swallow. After we swallow the food it goes to the stomach where there is hydrochloric acid which is the strongest acid that man knows. The stomach has bacteria that mixes with the hydrochloric acid to start the break down of the food that we have eaten. From there the food mixes with chemicals from the liver and the pancreas to turn into a mixture of chemicals that is called glucose. This glucose goes to red blood cells and the red blood cells go to the small intestines and then goes to the capillaries for the cells that are in the body to take on new food and give off waste.

The liquid waste goes to the kidnies and to the bladder and after exits the body. Solid waste exits the body through the large intestine and the bowels.

Now we learn about the Cardio Vascular System and how it works with the Digestive Track to keep our bodies alive. Mankind takes in to his lungs oxygen to mix with the blood in his body at the same time too he gives off Carbon Dioxide which is a by product of his motabolizium. The blood that has fresh oxygen in it carries the carries the glucoes from the food we eat to feed the other cells in the body

Now we will see in detail on how the Lungs and Heart operate the Cardio Vascular System. While the heart is in the first rest mode the Right Auracule is filling up with blood that has Carbon Dixoide from the body and that includes blood from the brain by the two viens on either side of the neck. At the same time there is blood with Carbon Dixoide in the Right Ventricule that has arrived on the first beat of the heart. On the second Heart beat the blood that is in the Right Ventricule goes to the lungs to give off Carbon Dixoide and take in Oxygen and the Right Ventricule is filled up with blood that has Carbon Dixoide from the Right Auracule and the blood that leaves the lungs with the fresh oxygen in it goes to the left auracule. Now at the same time the blood from the left auracule with oxygen in it goes to the brain by the two Arteries on the in side of the throat and the rest of the blood goes in to the Left Ventricule and to feed the chambers of the heart and the rest enters the body to mix with the Digestive Track.

So our bodies are nothing more than a group of individual organizums working together to keep the whole body alive as one. Most mammals are alive in this mannor. All life forms animated or non animated have sencors to tell them if the enviroment is changing slowly or suddenly in which case the life form can adapte to the enviroment. Some life forms have eyes which pick up radation on the retina at the back of their eyes and this radation stimilates the back of the eye with electrical impluses so the life form can form a picture or pictures like a movie around the life form's inviroment. If the life form does not have eyes it has feelers or wiskers that replace the eyes or both working together.

There are many substances that are no good for the body and our brain. The first is nicotine and is aquired by smoking cigarettes, and Canada is going to become a no smoking nation. There is grass and hash and hash oil other are cocaine power, horine power, rock, speed and shooting up cocaine and horine and speed. Another subsentance that is legal is alcohol which some times is abused

The first one cigarettes has 4,000 chemicals in the cigarette and one of those chemicals is nicotine which is called so because nicotine is a narcotic. How does this substance know a short cut to the brain doctors are looking for the answer is simple. When we exhale carbon dieoxide and we are taking in oxygen the nicotine from the cigarette goes into the left auricle and on the next beat of the heart all of the nicotine goes to the ten % of the brain that controls all automatic functions of the body.

The same thing applies to grass and hash. The powder cocaine and the powder horine the above also applies too. These also go to the ten % of the brain that controls all automatic functions of the body.

When you shoot up the illgeal drug goes to the right auricle on the first rest mode of the heart. Then after the first rest mode of the heart and on the first beat of the heart the right venterucle is filled with carbon dieoxide and what ever drug has been shot up. The there is a second rest mode of the heart and then the second heart beat the blood goes to the lungs to let off carbon dieoxide and take in fresh oxygen. While this happens the blood from the lungs goes into the left auricle containing illegal drug substances and after the third rest mode and on the third heart beat goes to the 10% of the brain that controls all automatic body funcutions.

Alcoholic's have a hard time controlling how much that they drink and it goes like this the Cardio Vasclar System makes a complete circulation of the body every twenty five minutes and if a person drinks one drink and twenty minutes later the alcohol does not have a chance to leave the body before the first drink effects and the alcohol effects build up and the person gets drunk. The alcohol also affects the 10 % of the brain that controlls all the automated movements of the body.

Now we see how alcohol is putting a big portion of the taxes that the Government collects to help alcoholic individuals help get over their illness but as I know from experience that no amount of medication will help these people as the ones that want to stop drinking are the ones that have made up their minds to stay sober the rest of their lives and do it without any medication.

Now with cigarettes if you get ill and go to a doctor he may perscribe some medication to make you better. But the nicotine from the cigarettes and other drugs changes the chemical make up of the medication and when you go back to the doctor for him to see the results of the medication that he perscribed for you did not work as well as a person that does not smoke as that person has no problem with nicotine or other drugs changing chemical make of the perscription around and the person that does not smoke will have a better check up percentage.

Now for grass and hash and hash oil the price is $ 15.00 dollars a gram. There are a lot of people in Canada and The U.S.A. that use these illegal drugs and at the above price The Governments of Canada and The U.S.A. can not keep pace with this amount of money through taxes to try and bring peace in the middle east and other spots in the world.

For cocaine powder and horine powder the price is $ 20.00 dollars a line and for rock the price is $ 20.00 dollars 1/4 gram or $ 80.00 dollars a gram. With these prices hopefully we can see that taxes for Canada and The U.S.A. can not keep up with illegal street drugs. After for a spoon of speed it is $ 20.00 dollars a spoon.

Where is all of this leading to is from the Middle East and Colombia the country in South America selling illegal drugs to the young while trying to take our freedom and rights away from us and our children by trying to make Dictorships and Comminisium. When they do landry the money it goes to China and Russia to make weapons to kill our soldiers over in the Middle East and in South America.

How the illegal drugs are distrubed in Canada and The U.S.A. Since organized crime has bought most legal business in the two countries it is easy for organized crime to pay customs cleck's to turn a blind eye and let the illegal drugs enter the two countries under raw materials. If these customs clerk's refuse to turn a blind eye their family members are brothered.

Once the illegal drugs get to the factory where the illegal drugs are seperated from the raw materials. The illegal drugs are taking to a motocycle gang where they are cut for street use. Anyone that wants illegal drugs is just to ask a friend who has smoked with them some hash. The person that takes the order calls a center with a cell phone to a pager and the center calls that person back on a pager telling the pusher what telephone number to call to order the illegal drugs and the pusher gives the order to the a peddle cycle boy who delievers the illegal drugs. Usally for one area there is about three to four workers in the center taking telephone numbers on pagers from pushers and calling back to the pusher to give the telephone number to order the illegal drugs. After the pusher gives the order and where to send the order to or address. With that being complete there is peddle cycle boy who is just a teenager with an amount a daily supply of illegal drugs and the pusher tells him how much and of what and the address to where the order is suppose to go. Once the boy collects the money he puts it in to three different bank accounts so if the police catch one gang member the police do not catch the other two. How is this money handled is some goes for weapons to kill anyone trying to stop this kind of business also a good portion goes to the organized crime to have a higher standard of living than most people. The rest goes in to stealing weapons developed in Canada and The U.S.A. to be shipped over to China and Russia so those two countries could distrube the weapons to countries in the Middle East. And at the same to the rest of the money for China and Russia to develope weapons that are better than the ones that were stolen from Canada and The U.S.A. by organized crime shipped over to those two countries.

How organized crime is ripping off Canada and The U.S.A. in gambling it is organized crime that bought into the Seven Sisters which are the seven oil companies in the world. And to do it organized crime had seven casino's in Las Vages. And we all know that if you gamble you lose your money and is just like an automatic money donation to organized crime. The owners of the casino's put the most expensive slot machines at the front and the smaller ones at the back.

What is organized crime into besides illegal drugs and owning the Seven Sisters so organized crime can charge what ever they want for gas for cars, well there is gambling, loan sharking, strip bars, prostition of young girls so they can get money to go to university after being hooked on illegal drugs, murder of people that stand up to organized crime, and all those crimes are on the rise daily and nightly.

Government Officials tell people if they go any where to stay with their friends so that they will not be attacked by a gang. That leads to gang wars you are better going by yourself and not making a scene or comment on other people's behavoir.

People think that there is a meaning for The Mafia that is kept a secret but in reality it only means organized crime then people will say what The Italian Mafia or The Japanese Mafia. The truth of the matter no matter where there is some one being afraid of The Mafia it boils down to one thing that it is a cover up word for organized crime.

Some meanings for the word MAFIA

Military Armed Forces In America

This group is the FBI and The Royal Mounted Police as well as other law enforcement officals in Canada and The U.S.A. trying to stop illegal drugs in both countries

Military Asian Forces In America

This group brings illegal drugs in to Canada and The U.S.A. when they immagrate to one or the other country or after settling here have their realitaves mail the illegal drugs to them

Man And Father In Anger

This group is about a father and his son who angry about one of them   being in the mafia or even the two of them being in the mafia

Mother And Father In Anger

this group is in anger over one of them being in the mafia or the two of them in the mafia and either a son or a daugther or both of them being in the mafia.

Mother And Father Italain Assocation

This group does favors for you and at any time they ask a favor from you.

People of The U.S.A. just call themselves United States Citizens and their Government is a Republic which means the government is responsable to the public this is partly true but excately it is a Democrate Republic as their Government is freely voted in which makes it Democrate and Republic the Government is responsable to the people.

Canada has a Federal Government which shares powers with the Provinces. In this type of arangement for the two different levels of Government of Canada being freely vote in and being responsable for the people makes Canada a Democrate Republic for both levels of Government.

China is a dictatorship and there are no freedoms for the people like we have here. As far as Russia goes They were first United Soverign Socialist Republic. Before the organized crime took it over it was rather easy as all the organized crime had to do was to put people in the Government of one the states and because it was considered Soverign and could tell the other states not to interfer with their Government and made the laws that concerned the perticular state as to how much money was going to each person so no one group could stand up to the new Government which was run discreately and formed The KGB and if some one made it in or was elected in to Government he was set up for a scandle and did a term in jail. All the other states in the U.S.S.R. were taken over this way.

In Canada we have The Royal Canadian Mounted Police and every one should be subjected to the laws of Canada even the Government. But in Canada we also have CSIS that can get ride of Government Officals by making a scandle even if it is true or not which is the same way that The U.S.S.R. was taken over by organized crime.

Another country that has this problem is The U.S.A. with the C.I.A. which can get ride of Government Officals if they do not like them. The proper way is that The F.B.I. inforces all people that break the laws of The U.S.A. including the Government other wise they too might be taken over by organized crime.

The last is England which has the I.S.I. which is like the CSIS in Canada and like the C.I.A. in The U.S.A.

What started World War 11. The European countries were trying to make a common currence to ward off an up coming inflation all the other countries said yes except Germany who invested their money with Israel and when Germany wanted their money back to put it with the European common currence. Israel told Germany that they could not have their money back and that they invested Germany's money in Russia which was run by organized crime.

Hilter want to take over Russia but had to go through Europe to get to Russia. And that is why Germany picked on the Jewish in World War 11.

When my father was born 1925 and my mother in 1926 there was a depression coming up but when my parents were 11 years old and 10 years old. They had comic books about a space man called Buck Rogers who had a rocket pack on his back and rocket boots on his feet and was traveling to other planets in space and they did not at the time think that it would come true but it did as it did in 1969 The United States of North America put a man on the moon by the name of Neil Armstrong. In the year that I was born in which was 1951 the U.S.A. government could pin point a cell phone any where in the world as soon it was turned on.

If we were lost in space and we did hit this planet that we call earth all the Television Vision Shows from the early 1960's and up to today's age have been themes about this subject but not in choronical order but ramdomly.

What the world needs now is stopping to create new wars and to stop all wars and put our resoures together like the International Space Station. So mankind can put people of their religion and customs on planets of their so that they and their young may live on in the future.

Now days The United States of North America has an aircraft carrier called The U.S.S. Enterprise and it is the largest aircraft carrier in the world. In the future their will be another U.S.S. Enterprise and it will belong to the S.F.F. The S.F.F. stands for Star Fleet Federation and the spaceship will be The United Star Ship Enterprise.

The space ship called The U.S.S. Enterprise will be able to travel faster than light as man already has T.V. and computer monitors run by electricty that send gamma rays to retina of the back of the human eye so these gamma rays stimolate the retina's of the eyes with electrical impulses to form pictures in our brains just like a movie.

Now you will see how to build the engines for Star Trek. The first thing is that all the outside of the spaceship must be built of strong solar panels. There would be a nulcar engines the solar panels would attract gamma waves to supply the nulcar engines with electrictity to work the computers on board the spaceship and there will be a cirrect breaker if an over load on the computers and if the computers lose their generators their will be an emergency generator with an over ride on the computers and if that fails their will be a centrealized computer that is programmed to do the work of the all the other computers put together on the emergency generator.

With the two above paragraphs now if we take two magnets a north pole and a south pole and we put them together then take a bigger two magnets with a north pole and a south pole. After we would wrap the outer magnets with electrical wire's in such way that it would take the two inner magnets and change them to north pole and north pole which rejects and south pole and south pole which rejects. In the process of doing this you must keep in mind that the outer magnets must remain north pole to south pole. Afterwards you can put a cover of a conductor over the two outer magnets with a joy stick to help stir the spaceship. This type of syncronized engines with the solar panels would get the nessary electricty to power the nulcar engines which in turn would feed gamma waves to the magnets in divisions of ten to attract gamma waves from stars transmitting electrical impulses from gravity pull from the star that the spaceship was heading to and based on the size of the star would help determind the warp speed. These engines would be like only engines that work in space as they run on nature of space and do not need to propel themselves like other feuls that could be a high explosive material. High explosive engines are more dangerous to operate than the ones I explained as there is nothing to propel explosive fuel on in space.

Now for the type of computers you would have would be microsoft windows as if a genernator fails there would be an aux generator would put up another window with the same program as every program would have dupulatict programs to take over the original program until the old generator could be fixed and the original program could be up and running again. For the speed of the spacecraft the computers would have to run at 186,000 miles per second and be generated up to ten times

This is a navigional system now when we read most numbers we start at the left and go to the right an exmaple of this is 624,368,273 as you notice the 6 is on the left which is the largest after at the 3 it is the lowest. The system works like this 1.000005297438 the number 1. stands for our sun or our star to plot a courase we start with the number one.five zero's five million two hundred and ninty seven thousand four hundred and and thirty eight but rather is called out like one.five two nine seven four three eight. Now the 1 stands for our sun and the five zero's stand for future stars going to be explored and the

5297438 for the number of stars that have been explored.

The next star being explored and it's solar system would be 1.000005297439.

And as more stars and their solar systems are being explored some of the numbers would be as follows 1.000005297440.

Another exampleis 1.000100000000 the next number would be 1.000100000001 anther example would be 1.953868425728 as you notice the one on the left side of the decemical never changes because all you have to do to get back home is to back track on the numbers on the right side of the decemical.

Yes for star dates the captain of a space ship would something like the following it would start with the star number and the number of planets and the moons of those planets that have life on them for that solar system. An example of this would be 683/4/7

The 683 would be the number star being explored and the number 4 would stand the number of planets in that solar system having life on them. The number 7 would stand for the moons of the planets having life on them as well as maybe moons just having life on them.

With space being so vast it is nessacary to have star bases so this method will support the nesscary equiment to navigate through the stars.

Just one more thing when traveling faster than light for an example if you are traveling at warp 4 you will need a radar front that would be 8 times ahead of your crusing speed warp speed to stop the space ship in case of an emergency or if you are doing warp 7 you will need radar at 14 ahead of your crusing speed

The two warp engines will have to be syncronized just like a dual cassette on a boom box for recording.

Written By Mark Derrick Boisvert

M. D. B.

www.ingramcontent.com/pod-product-compliance
Lightning Source LLC
Chambersburg PA
CBHW080356290526
45791CB00009BA/2891